CAMBRIDGE

PLAYWAY

to English

Second edition

1

Activity Book

with CD-ROM

Günter Gerngross

Herbert Puchta

HELBLING LANGUAGES

Contents

Unit 6: Weather

Structures
It's raining/snowing/sunny/windy/cloudy.
The little caterpillar is asleep/happy.
(The caterpillar) grows and grows.
Look at the wonderful (butterfly).

Vocabulary
rain, sun, wind, clouds, snow
raining, snowing, sunny, windy
butterfly, seed, flower

Unit 7: Party

Structures
What colour is number (one)?
Is number six (blue)?
Is this your cat?
Look at the cat.

Vocabulary
nine, ten
sheriff, princess, bear,
clown, crocodile, ghost, frog,
monster, magician, bird

Unit 8: Health

Structures
Have a (glass of milk).
It's healthy/unhealthy.
I feel sick.

Vocabulary
Get out of bed. Wash your face.
Clean your teeth. Have an apple.
Run to school. Sing a song.
My tooth hurts. Open your mouth.
Come in. Take a seat.
orange, chocolate, lolly

Unit 9: Food

Structures
(Chicken) is great.
What do you like?
I like (apples), (pears) and (bananas).

Vocabulary
butter, spaghetti, chicken, cheese, chips,
ketchup, cornflakes, milk, cake

Unit 10: Animals

Structures
How many (red) (elephants) are there?
Is it the (lion)?
It's the (duck).

Vocabulary
lion, elephant, monkey, snake, hippo

1 Look and say. Colour Linda, Benny and Max.

2 CD 1 6 Listen and tick (✓).

3 **Listen and colour.**

①

②

③

④

4  **Say and colour.**

5 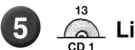 **Listen and colour.**

6 **Look and colour. Say.**

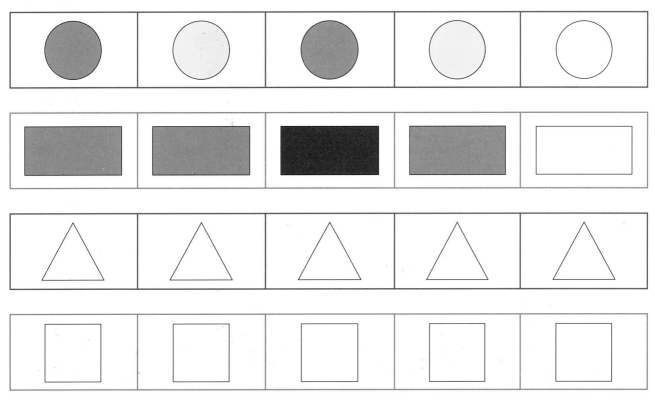

7  Listen and tick (✓).

1
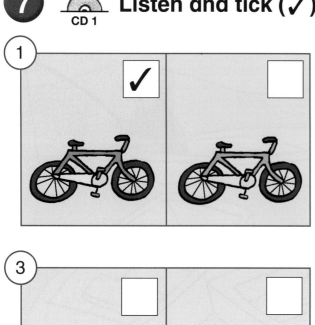

2
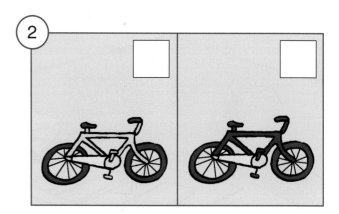

3
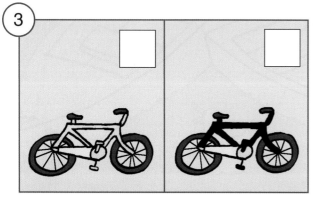

4
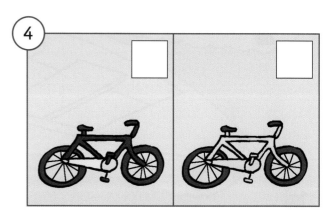

8 Look and colour.

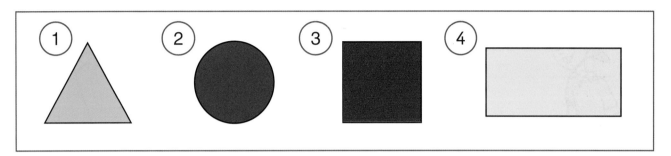

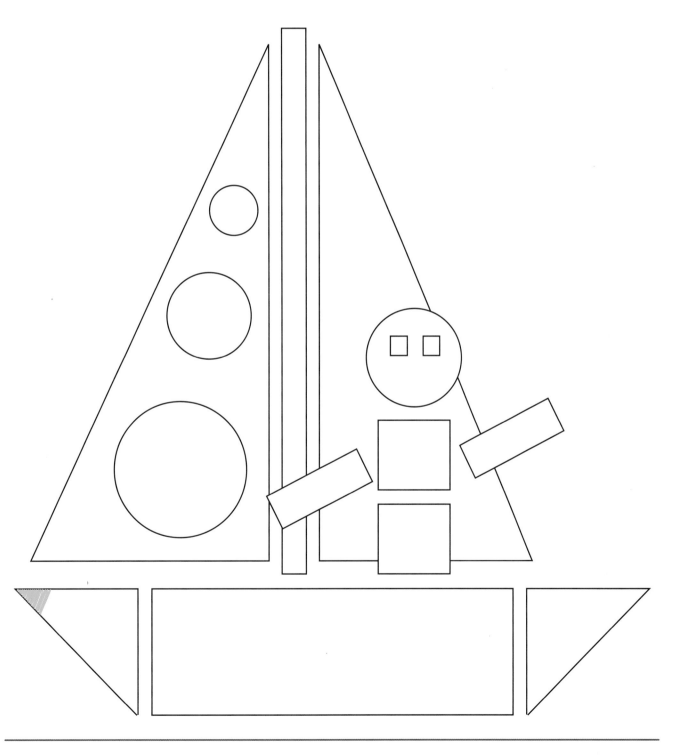

School

1 Colour and say.

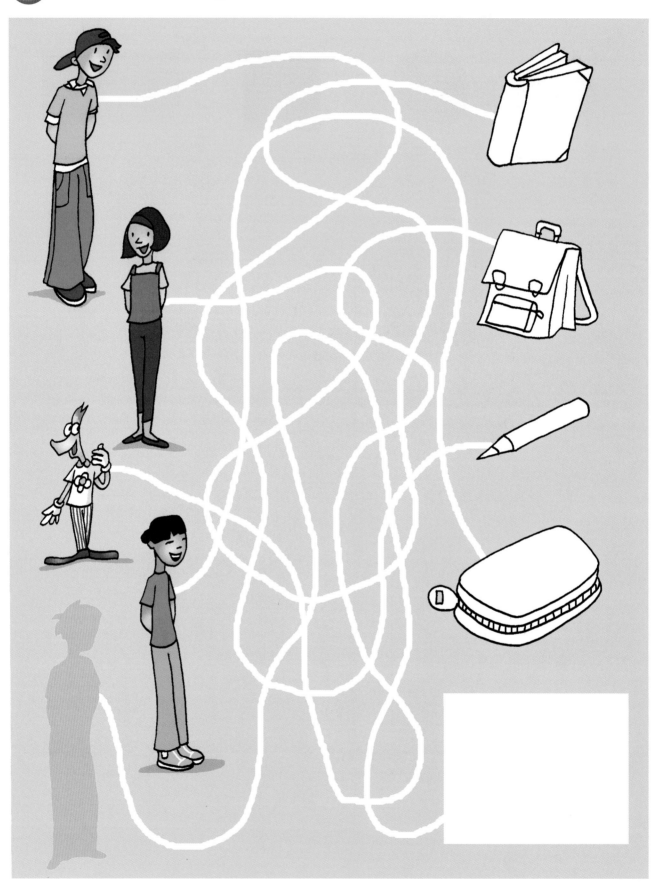

2 Listen and write the numbers.

17
CD 1

1

3 21 CD 1 **Listen and colour.**

4  **Listen and write the numbers.**

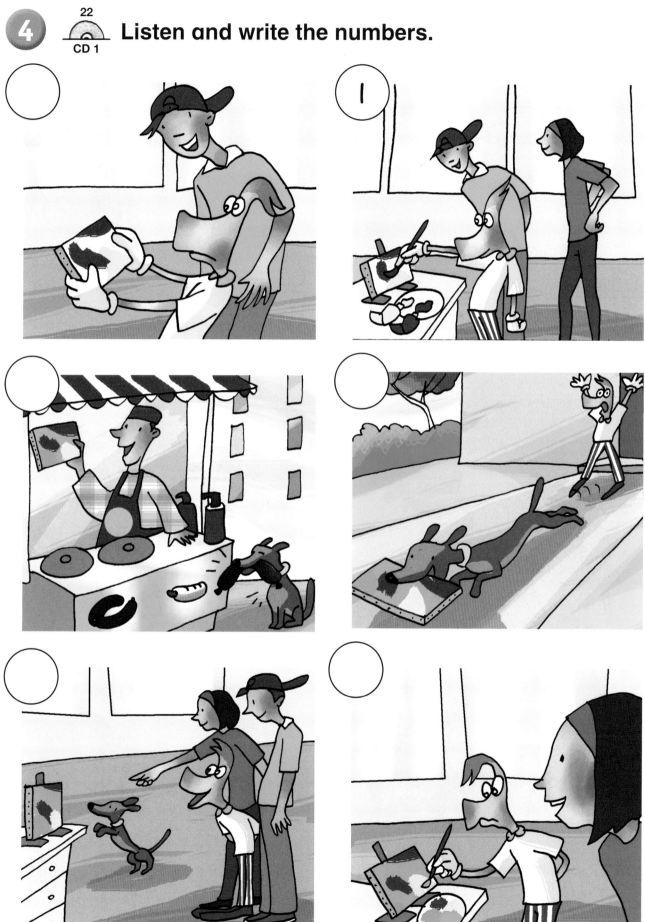

5

Listen and tick (✓).

6 Look and remember. Say.

7 Colour and say.

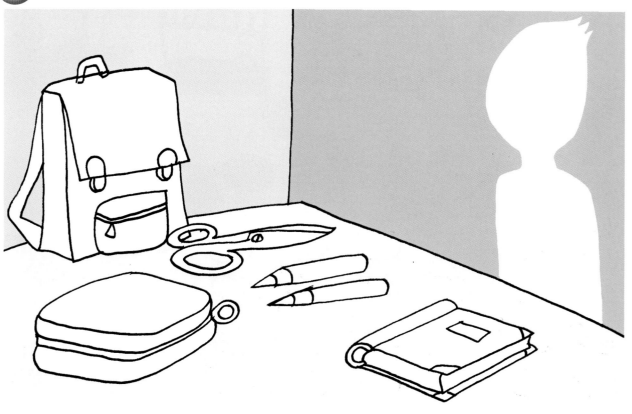

Fruit

1 Think and draw.

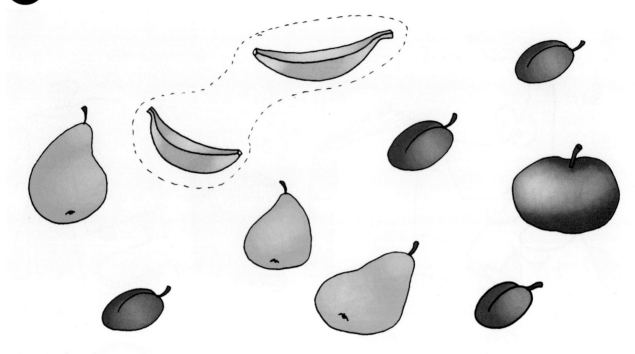

2 Count, colour and say.

3  31 CD 1 **Listen and tick (✓).**

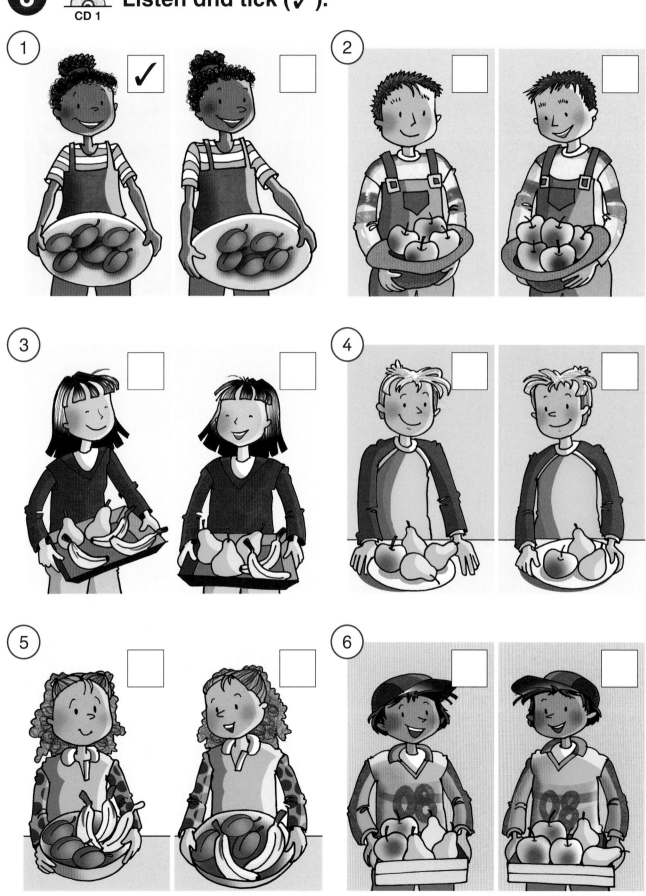

35
CD 1

4 Listen and write the numbers.

(1)

5  **Listen and draw.**

1

2

3

4

5

6

6 CD 1 39 **Listen and write the numbers.**

1

7 Do the sums. Say.

1 + 3 =	4	2 + 2 =		1 + 5 =	

2 + 3 =		1 + 4 =		4 + 2 =	

3 + 3 =		5 + 1 =		4 + 1 =	

3 + 2 =		1 + 1 =		2 + 1 =	

8 Look and colour. Say.

Pets

1 **Look and colour. Listen and point.**

2 **Look and write the numbers.**

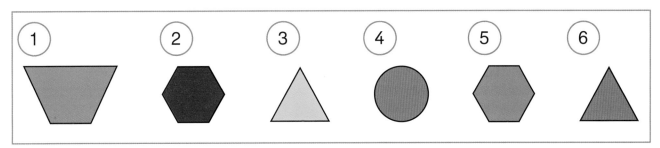

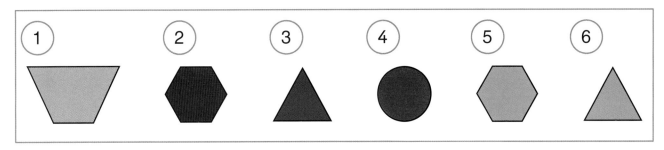

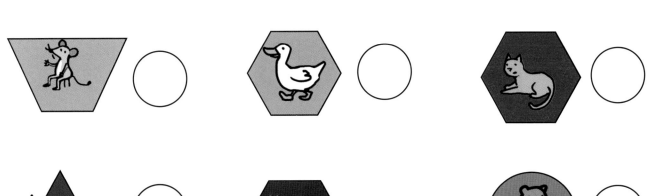

3 **Look and draw.**

  **4** **Draw.**

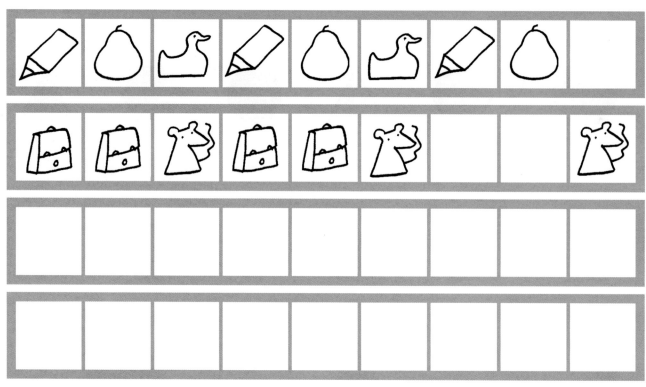

5 **Listen and tick (✓).**

CD 2   6

4

6 8 CD 2 **Listen and write the numbers.**

1

Unit 4

7 CD 2 · 9 **Listen and draw.**

1

2

3

4

27

Toys

1 **Look and colour. Count and write the numbers.**

2 **Listen and colour. Find, write the numbers and colour.**

1

2

3

4

5

6

7

8

3  **Listen and circle.**

1

2

4 Listen and tick (✓).

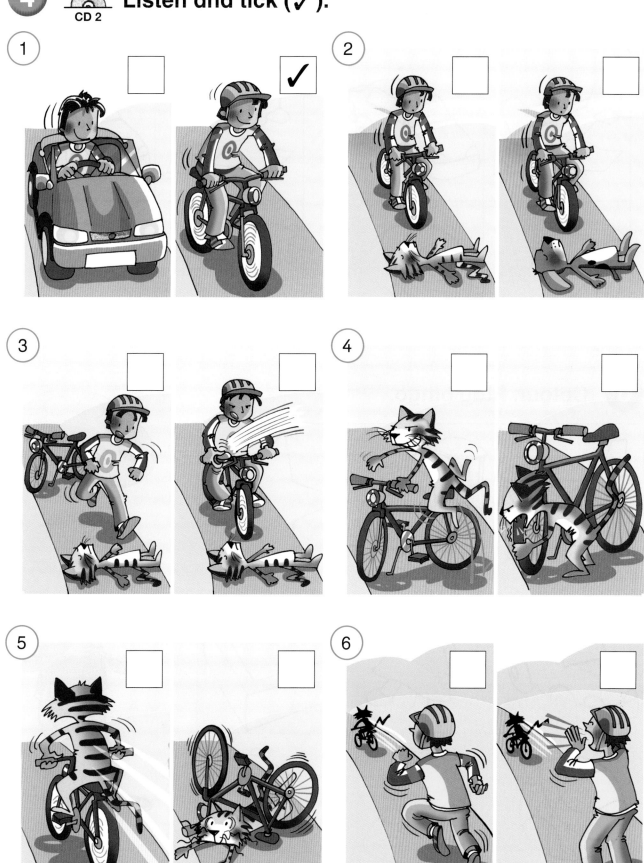

5 Colour and say.

1
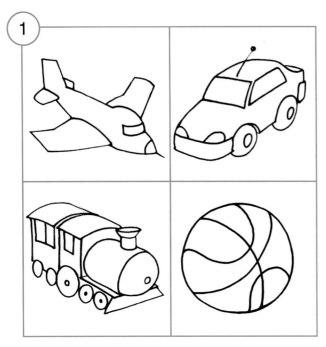

2
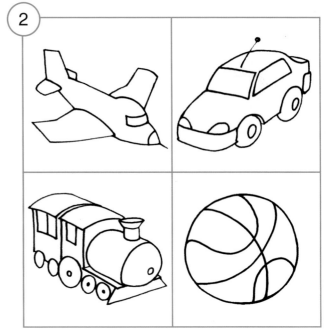

6 Colour. Play bingo.

7 Listen and circle.

1

2

8 Draw, colour and say.

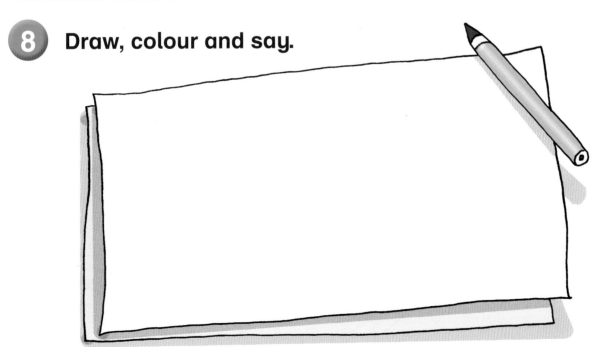

Weather

1 **Draw to complete the pictures. Say.**

①

②

③

④

⑤

2 **Listen and colour. Count and write the numbers.**

CD 2

Unit 6

3 | 31 CD 2 | **Listen and tick (✓).**

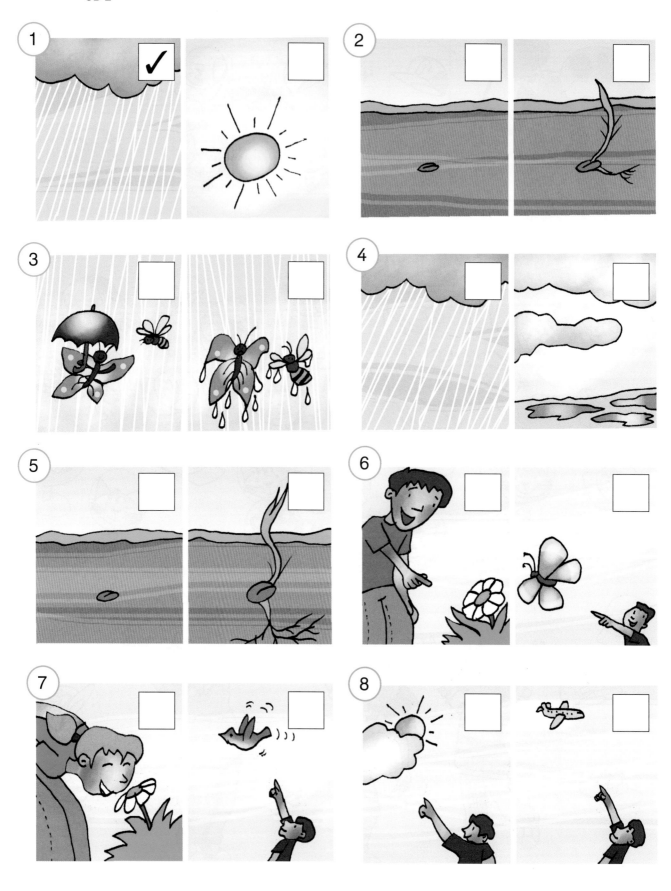

4 35 · CD 2 · **Listen and write the numbers.**

1

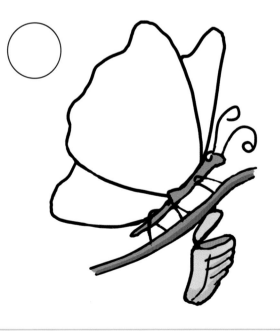

5 Look and draw. Say.

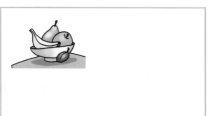

6 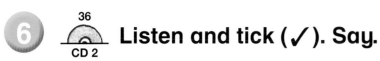 **Listen and tick (✓). Say.**

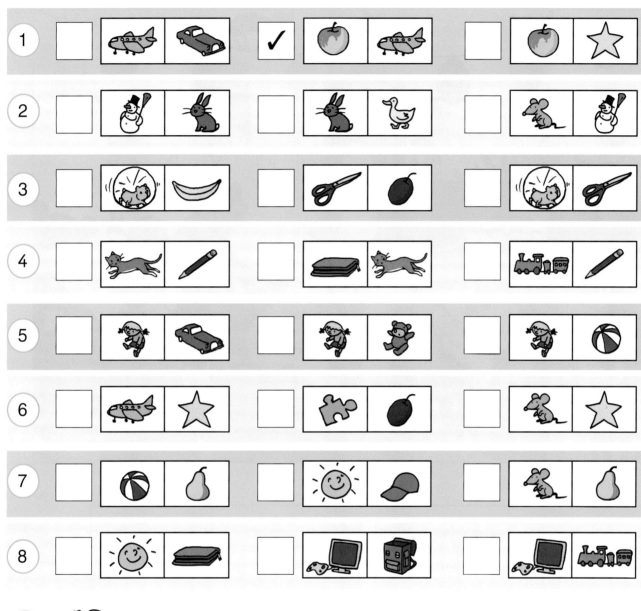

7 **Draw and say.**

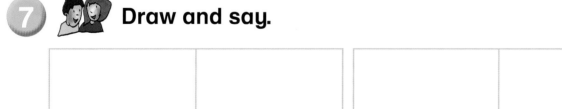

Party

1 CD 3 **Look and colour. Listen and check.**

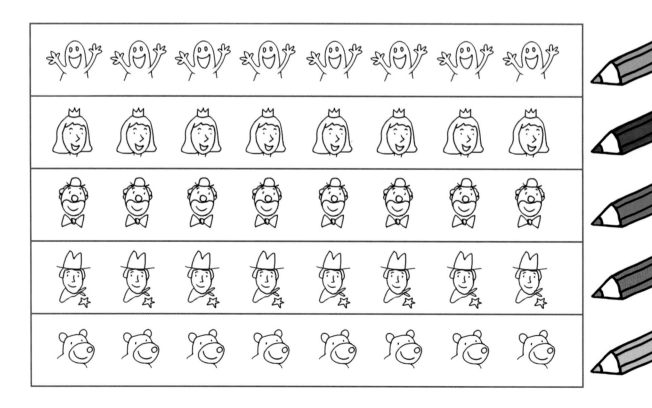

2 CD 3 4 **Listen and tick (✓).**

1

2

3 **Colour and say.**

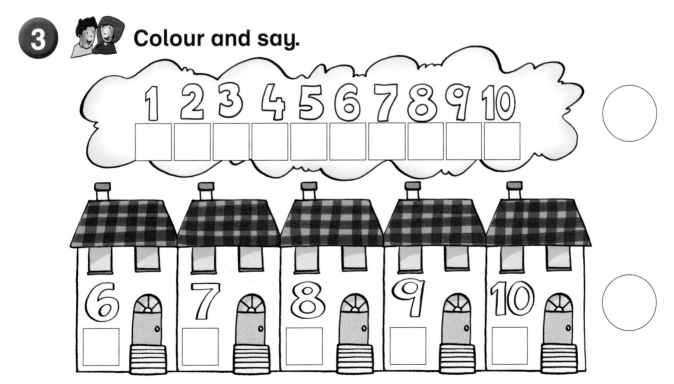

Unit 7

Listen and tick (✓).

42

5 **Listen and write the numbers.**

CD 3

6 Do the sums. Say.

2 + 7 = 9	1 + 6 =	6 + 3 =
8 + 1 =	5 + 2 =	4 + 3 =
3 + 6 =	4 + 1 =	3 + 5 =
7 + 2 =	4 + 2 =	4 + 5 =

7 11 CD 3 Listen and complete the picture.

8 **Listen and colour.**

Health

1 Listen and write the numbers.

1

2 Listen and tick (✓).
CD 3

1

2

3

4

5

6

  3 19 CD 3 **Listen and write the numbers.**

1

1

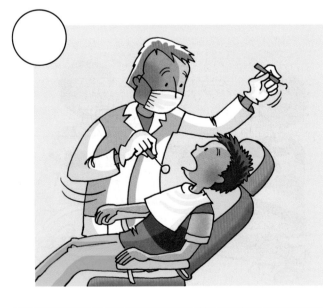

Think and draw. Say.

5  **Listen and write the numbers.**

CD 3 — 22

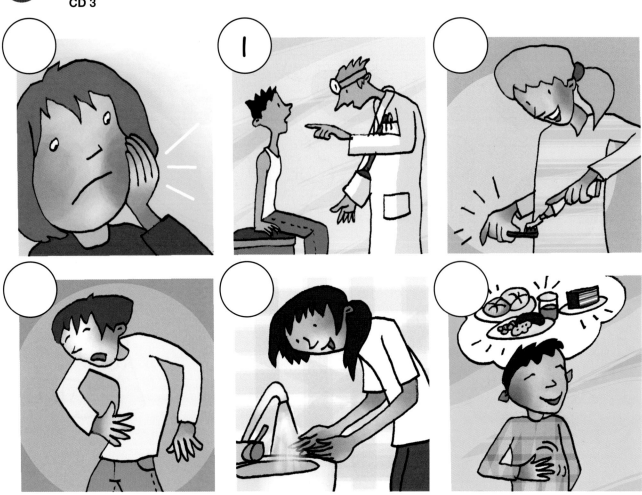

6 **Say and mime.**